Photographing Your Vacation

Read *Photographing Your Vacation* and learn how to—

- Travel safely with your camera equipment and film.

- Handle a variety of lighting and weather conditions.

- Spot and record unique and exotic situations.

- Take the types of photographs that accurately record treasured memories.

THE NO NONSENSE LIBRARY

OTHER NO NONSENSE PHOTOGRAPHY GUIDES

Composing Photographs
Photographing People
Using Accessory Equipment
Using Creative Techniques
Using Existing Light

OTHER NO NONSENSE GUIDES

Car Guides
Career Guides
Cooking Guides
Financial Guides
Health Guides
Legal Guides
Parenting Guides
Real Estate Guides
Study Guides
Success Guides
Wine Guides

NO NONSENSE PHOTOGRAPHY GUIDE™

PHOTOGRAPHING YOUR VACATION

A KODAK Book

ERIN HENNESSEY

Longmeadow Press

PHOTOGRAPHING YOUR VACATION

Published by Longmeadow Press, 201 High Ridge Road, Stamford, Connecticut 06904. No part of this book may be reproduced or used in any form or by any means, electronic or mechanical, including photocopying, recording, or by an information storage and retrieval system, without permission in writing from the publisher.

No Nonsense Photography Guide is a trademark controlled by Longmeadow Press.

ISBN 0-681-40733-6

Copyright © 1990 by The Image Bank, Inc.

Produced by The Image Bank in association with Eastman Kodak Company, Rochester, New York.

Kodak is a registered trademark of Eastman Kodak Company and is used under license from Kodak.

The Image Bank® is a registered trademark of The Image Bank, Inc.

Printed in Spain

0 9 8 7 6 5 4 3 2 1

Producer: Solomon M. Skolnick; *Managing Editor:* Elizabeth Loonan; *Editors:* Terri Hardin (The Image Bank), Margaret Buckley (Kodak); *Production Director:* Charles W. Styles (Kodak); *Production Coordinator:* Ann-Louise Lipman (The Image Bank); *Editorial Assistant:* Carol Raguso; *Production Assistant:* Valerie Zars; *Photo Researchers:* Natalie Goldstein, Lenore Weber; *Copy Editor:* Irene S. Korn; *Art Direction and Design:* Chase/Temkin & Associates, Inc.

Cover photographs, left to right: Janeart, Robert Phillps, David W. Hamilton

For information about the photographs in this book, please contact:
The Image Bank
111 Fifth Avenue
New York, NY 10003

TABLE OF CONTENTS

INTRODUCTION

Vacations are the perfect time to take pictures. They offer you the leisure and locations to experiment with new subjects and techniques. But how often have you been disappointed with your vacation photos? There you were, in that beautiful setting, shooting to your heart's content. But when the photos came back from the lab, they were underexposed, overexposed, or out of focus. What went wrong?

Ask yourself a few key questions: Do I know how my camera works? Did I take the right kind of film? The answers to these questions will help determine if you really gave yourself a chance.

Photographing Your Vacation will show you how planning your photos and a good understanding of your camera and its accessories can improve your photos dramatically. We'll review a few photographic rules of thumb, such as packing camera equipment and film correctly, tips on shooting problem locations, and most important, how to get your friends and family "in the picture." We'll also look at some strong location photographs taken by photographers who really put a lot of care into capturing the moment.

Photos of your vacation are unique treasures; they preserve the priceless memories of the time you've spent relaxing with your family or friends, or even by yourself. The sights you've seen, the places you've traveled, and the experiences you've had will always be within easy reach when you take your camera with you. The tips you will find in this book and the experience you will gain as you take more pictures will help you produce photographs that will capture the essence of your vacation.

Read through this book carefully, and study the photographs that most appeal to you for techniques you can use in your own photography. Check the glossary in the back of the book for terms you're unfamiliar with. Important terms are in italics throughout the book and are listed in the glossary. The following pages will inspire you and give you the confidence to photograph your next vacation with ease, enjoyment, and the best possible results!

PART ONE

BEFORE YOUR
VACATION

Terje Rakke

Whether it's having enough traveler's checks or packing an extra battery for your camera, planning for a trip always pays off, and so does a bit of picture-taking practice.

The more pictures you take before your vacation, the better your vacation photos will be. This is particularly true if you have recently purchased a camera or haven't used your camera for months.

First, shoot a roll or two of film to get back into the swing of things. Then look over your pictures carefully while the picture-taking situations are still fresh in your mind. Using this book as your guide, examine lighting, focus, and composition as separate elements. This will give you a good idea of what you need to work on. Shoot another roll, and see if you can correct your mistakes.

Do this before your trip, and your camera will feel like an old friend by the time you hit the road or resort. Isn't that better than grabbing your camera at the last minute with the desperate hope that you'll get lucky and everything will fall into place by the time you push the button?

Where are you going? A little research before you begin your vacation will not only work to your advantage as a tourist but will also help you decide what type of film to take along. Ask yourself such questions as "What will the climate be like? Can I expect a lot of sun, or will I be indoors most of the time?"

If you know, for instance, that you are going to a sunny beach for a week, think about what kind of film you'll need for that type of location. The beach means bright sunlight, with a lot of light reflecting off both sand and water. You'll want a film that's not too fast, such as KODACOLOR GOLD 100 Film. If you can use a filter over your camera lens, you may also want to take a polarizing filter to reduce glare. A polarizing filter will also help you capture striking, deep-blue skies.

Also think photography when you pack your clothes. If you plan to be outside at the crack of dawn to photograph the sunrise, you'll want to take some warm clothes along. And what about rainy days? You won't have to stay indoors if you take

Before you go on vacation, take time to get reacquainted with your camera. Practice taking pictures of people and places, and be sure to experiment with your exposure controls.

along some rainwear. You can spend your afternoons taking shots of subjects such as parks, skylines, and rocky seashores that look beautiful in the rain.

Check with your insurance agent to make sure your photographic equipment is covered if it's lost or stolen. Homeowner's and renter's insurance often cover your camera and other equipment even when you take them on vacation, but verifying this will put your mind at ease.

Here's a checklist to get you started on planning your trip. You may want to add to this list, but don't subtract! The answers to these questions are vital if you want to be prepared.

PHOTOGRAPHING YOUR VACATION

PACKING YOUR EQUIPMENT

If you want to take a lot of pictures, then pack your camera equipment so that it's always convenient to use and easy to get to.

Keep all your photo gear together. This means not only your camera body, but extra lenses and filters, an extra battery (or two), flash units, cleaning supplies (lens tissue and cleaning fluid), and if possible, a receipt for your camera, in case you are questioned about where you purchased the camera while going through customs.

When you're flying, it's always a good idea to pack all your photo equipment in your carry-on luggage. Make sure your camera bag is well padded. Carrying your equipment will protect it from loss or damage if your other luggage is lost, stolen, or simply mishandled. In addition to these practical advantages, having your camera gear with you gives you the opportunity to take some spectacular pictures from the air! (See pages 55 and 56 for tips on photographing from the airplane.)

Another hint: No matter how well you know your camera, take the manual along. Vacations are a good time to experiment with your equipment and test features that you may have ignored or felt intimidated by in the past.

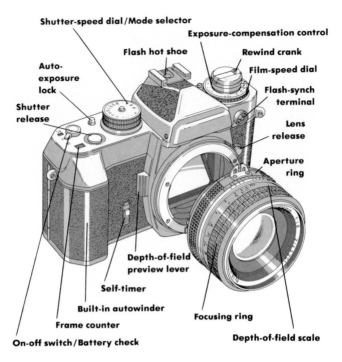

Shutter-speed dial/Mode selector

Exposure-compensation control

Flash hot shoe

Rewind crank

Film-speed dial

Auto-exposure lock

Flash-synch terminal

Shutter release

Lens release

Aperture ring

Depth-of-field preview lever

Self-timer

Built-in autowinder

Focusing ring

Frame counter

On-off switch/Battery check

Depth-of-field scale

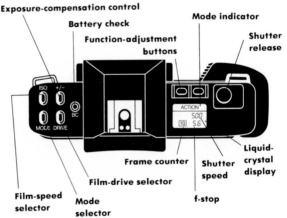

Exposure-compensation control

Battery check

Function-adjustment buttons

Mode indicator

Shutter release

ACTION
500
10 5.6

Frame counter

Shutter speed

Liquid-crystal display

Film-drive selector

Film-speed selector

Mode selector

f-stop

Some cameras allow you to adjust controls such as the film-speed setting, aperture, and shutter speed.

TAKING FILM OR BUYING IT THERE

Figure out how much film you'll need for your vacation—then double it! And always buy film before leaving home. That way you'll be sure to have what you want on hand. Otherwise, you may have to choose from a limited and often more expensive selection, particularly if you end up in a remote place or a tourist area.

When choosing your film, think flexibility. You may be going to a sunny place, but what about those beautiful shade and night scenes, not to mention all those indoor pictures that you'll want to shoot?

Chances are, you'll be taking most of your pictures under normal daylight conditions. Whether you choose print or slide

If you plan to do a lot of indoor sight-seeing, remember to take along a fast film to handle low-light situations.

Brett Froomer

Frank Whitney

film, color or black-and-white film, be sure to pack plenty of medium-speed film (ISO 64 to 200). Use films that are slower or faster than this as described below:

FILMS FOR DIFFERENT LIGHTING LEVELS

- High-speed films (ISO 250 to 640), such as KODACOLOR GOLD 400 and KODAK EKTACHROME 400 Films, are for use in lower light levels. These films also let you use higher shutter speeds to stop action, or smaller lens openings to increase *depth of field*. (For an explanation of depth of field, see page 37 or the glossary.)
- Very-high-speed films (ISO 800 to 1600), such as KODACOLOR GOLD 1600 and KODAK EKTAR 1000 Films, are best in very dim light, to stop fast action, or for greater versatility with telephoto or zoom lenses.
- Low-speed films (ISO 50 or lower), such as KODAK EKTAR 25 and KODACHROME 25 Films, work best for taking sharp pictures in bright light.

Outdoors, a medium-speed film can handle a wide range of lighting situations, such as sunsets, ski and beach scenes, and typical scenics.

Janeart Ltd.

Kaz Mori

15

When you buy the films you've decided on, check the "Process before" date on the box.

AIRPORT X-RAY INSPECTION

You may see signs at X-ray inspection stations in airports that say "will not harm film." Perhaps one scan won't hurt, but the effects of X-ray exposure are cumulative. Repeated low-level X-ray exposures can fog unprocessed film (exposed or unexposed) and produce "ghost" images of items in your luggage on the film. High-speed and very-high-speed films are especially sensitive to X-rays.

It's always a good idea to ask for a visual inspection of your camera as well as all of your exposed and unexposed film when you're going through airport security. It may not always be possible, but at least it will cut down on the number of times your film is X-rayed. Carrying your film in a clear plastic bag will speed up and simplify the visual inspection.

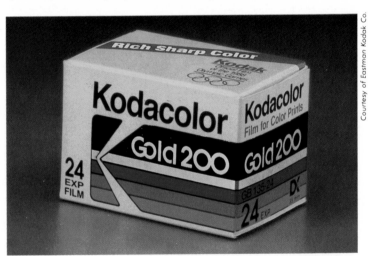

Courtesy of Eastman Kodak Co.

Kodak makes a number of medium-speed films that are suitable for many lighting situations. KODACOLOR GOLD 200 Film is one of the most popular films for prints.

PHOTOGRAPHING YOUR VACATION

Bill Carter

To produce a silhouette effect with a backlit subject, base your exposure on the brighter background illumination.

Thomas R. Rampy III

Try to capture the essence of your vacation spot, whether it is the romance of an ancient city or the tranquility of a country hideaway.

PHOTOGRAPHING YOUR VACATION

Matthew Loonan

PROCESSING YOUR FILM

It's always a good idea to take processing mailers with you so that you can mail your exposed film for processing while you are still away. This will help to minimize exposure to X-ray scanners if you are flying from place to place, and it will lighten your load as you go along. If you plan to be gone for a long time, you might want to arrange for the processing lab to mail your processed film back to a friend at home for safe-keeping until you return. If you mail film in packages other than processing mailers, label them "Undeveloped Film. Do Not X-ray. Protect From Heat and Radioactive Materials."

The less exposed film you have to worry about, the better. Storing it in a cool, dry place is not always easy when you are traveling. So the sooner you can send it off for processing, the better. And always have your film processed before the "Process before" date printed on the film carton.

If you decide to process your film while you are "on location" outside the U.S., it would be a good idea to write to Kodak for a list of their processing labs. Write to Kodak Information Center, Eastman Kodak Company, Rochester, New York 14650-0811.

PHOTOGRAPHING PEOPLE AND PLACES

Butch Martin

When you decide to take a vacation, so many destinations are open to you: the beach, the tropics, mountains, parks—to name just a few. And since each location has specific conditions that can affect your photography, you can't always apply the same rules and expect the same results.

In Part Two, we'll discuss how to photograph your loved ones on vacation, as well as how to get the best pictures of your surroundings, even when the conditions aren't ideal.

YOU AND YOUR FAMILY

Most people think that photographing their families in a vacation setting is really the point of taking pictures on vacation. It's a way of giving one's family a sense of shared experience, and offers opportunities for many candid shots of family members interacting (with greater or lesser success!) in the vacation environment.

When you take pictures of the family, the first rule of thumb is *don't forget yourself!* Too often, the photographer gets left out completely because he or she is always behind the camera. Make sure a friend or member of your family takes some pictures of you too.

Remember to direct your family with a light touch. Travelers can sometimes be strained by missed connections or crowded accommodations. Not everyone will be in a good mood during some of the picture-taking. Be sensitive to this: a kind word at the right moment may save you from those forced smiles that are just as bad as scowls. Make sure your subjects are in relaxed positions; whenever possible, try to take unposed pictures. Those slice-of-life moments will tell the story of your trip.

You'll need to use a fast *shutter speed* to capture kids in action and other spontaneous fun. The shutter speed controls *how long* your film is exposed to light, and using a fast shutter speed—such as 1/500 second—means that the light entering your camera through the lens opening *(aperture)* strikes your film for only a short time.

PEOPLE AND PLACES

Lisl Dennis

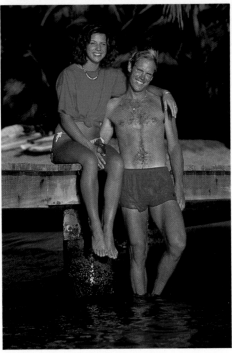

Melchior DiGiacomo

Don't leave yourself out of the picture. The self-timer on your camera will let you make shots such as the photograph above. Or set the camera controls and ask someone to take a picture of you.

With a zoom lens, you can shoot from a distance and still get in the middle of the action without disturbing your subject or risking damage to your camera.

To expose your film to the correct amount of light, you should understand how shutter speed and aperture control exposure. The most commonly used shutter speeds are fractions of a second, such as 1/60, 1/125, and 1/250. These fractions are marked on your camera shutter-speed dial as 60, 125, and 250. Aperture controls *how much* light strikes the film while the shutter is open. Apertures are expressed as *f-numbers* or *f-stops,* such as $f/2.8$, $f/4$, $f/5.6$, $f/8$, $f/11$, $f/16$, and $f/22$.

If you have a manually adjustable camera or an automatic camera that you can use in a manual mode, experiment with different combinations of shutter speed and aperture to see what is best for the situations you expect to encounter. You can use the chart on page 24 as a guide to setting the proper exposure.

SUGGESTED DAYLIGHT EXPOSURES

LIGHTING	ISO 100	ISO 200	ISO 400	ISO 1000	ISO 1600
Bright or hazy sun on sand or snow	f/16 1/250	f/16 1/500	f/16 1/1000	f/22 1/1000	f/22 1/2000
Bright or hazy sun (distinct shadows)	f/16 1/125	f/16 1/250	f/16 1/500	f/16 1/1000	f/22 1/1000
Weak, hazy sun (soft shadows)	f/11 1/125	f/11 1/250	f/11 1/500	f/11 1/1000	f/16 1/1000
Cloudy-bright (no shadows)	f/8 1/125	f/8 1/250	f/8 1/500	f/8 1/1000	f/11 1/1000
Open shade or heavy overcast	f/5.6 1/125	f/5.6 1/250	f/5.6 1/500	f/5.6 1/1000	f/8 1/1000

Note: With ISO 64 film, increase the exposures suggested for ISO 100 film by one stop, i.e., use the next larger lens opening or the next slower shutter speed.

It's not always easy to make an effective group shot with your subject far from you if you're using a normal lens (e.g., 50 mm for a 35 mm camera). If you stand back far enough to get all the people in, they become too small. But if you get in too close, you may cut off the people at the edges of the group.

You can solve this problem by using a wide-angle lens. It covers a wider field of view than a normal lens. If you don't have a wide-angle lens, you can try shooting down from a ladder, a staircase, or even a low balcony. (You don't want the balcony to be too high, or your group will look small.) Or you can put your group on the balcony and shoot from the ground. These types of angles will accommodate more people than the straight-on approach.

David W. Hamilton

In this picture, a wide-angle lens was used to include all family members in the shot. If you don't want to carry many lenses while traveling, take along a zoom lens that covers a good range of focal lengths.

If you're using flash to photograph people scattered about a room, remember that any object closer than the minimum flash range will be washed out by the bright light of the flash. See your camera or flash manual for the recommended flash range. This is a particular problem with fully automatic cameras that have a strong built-in flash. Several subjects at different distances from the camera will receive different amounts of light (some will be too light, and others too dark). To avoid this, arrange all your subjects at roughly the same distance from the flash.

Do your pictures of people often come back from the lab with all your subjects' eyes glowing red? The old problem of red-eye can turn an attractive picture into a ghoulish scene. The red is actually a reflection of the flash from blood vessels in the

Off-camera bounce flash casts an even, diffused light on your subject and the surrounding area, creating a more natural look than the harsh flattening effect of direct on-camera flash.

---

back of the eye. To prevent red-eye, turn on all available room lights. The extra brightness will help contract your subjects' pupils and reduce reflections. Increasing the distance between the flash and camera lens also helps. If possible, remove the flash from the camera or use an extender to increase the angle between lens and flash.

Bouncing your flash off the ceiling or wall will also help prevent red-eye. Remember that with color film, the bounce surface should be white to avoid a color cast; you'll also need a larger aperture to compensate for the increased flash-to-subject distance and the light lost by absorption and scattering.

This procedure will work only if you have a flash unit that can be tilted or separated from the camera body. With your camera focused on your subject, aim your flash at the ceiling or a nearby wall. When the unit fires, the flash will bounce off the ceiling or wall and illuminate your subject with soft, diffuse light.

PHOTOGRAPHING YOUR VACATION

BEACHES

Beaches are great vacation spots, but we often underestimate the intensity of the sun—whether we're sunbathing or taking pictures! If you're going to be baking on the beach, make sure your camera isn't baking with you! Keep it covered and in a shaded place when you're not using it. And when you're taking pictures, be sure to shield your camera from sea spray and flying sand. Of course, you can't shield it all the time, so remember to wipe off your lens each evening with a fresh piece of lens tissue.

Keep your extra film cool as well. If possible, take along a small cooler, such as a light-colored, padded 6-can (soda/beer) picnic pack, packed with blue plastic ice squares. You can put the plastic ice holders into an ice machine in your hotel overnight, which should keep them cold for about 48 hours.

Elyse Lewin

Sand and water reflect a lot of light and can cause your camera to underexpose your subject. To avoid silhouettes of your family on the beach, take a close-up meter reading.

James H. Carmichael, Jr.

By concentrating on the details around you, you can add another dimension to your vacation pictures. Here, the photographer used a large aperture to throw the surrounding elements out of focus, adding impact to the sharp angles of the shell.

A lot of people find beaches simply overwhelming as photo subjects. It isn't surprising; beaches are tricky when it comes to lighting and composition. They look so vast and horizontal at first glance, with so much sand and water!

For these reasons you should carefully plan each picture. By concentrating on each element separately, you can get over the feeling that this subject is "too much."

Look at all the shapes, patterns, and colors around you, and don't forget the fascinating textures provided by wet sand, palm-tree bark, and barnacle-covered rocks. Try photographing a wave breaking against the shore, or a shadow cast by a palm tree. Most of all, analyze why you're struck by a particular scene, and then set your exposure carefully. (For tips on exposure, see page 24.)

Ask yourself if the time of day gives you the light you're looking for. If you're staying in one location awhile, you might want to take a day to observe how the light changes as the hours pass.

The well-composed photograph above combines the large horizontal expanse of sand and water with a vertical portrait of the family and their reflections. This leads the eye all around the image and then returns it to the main subject.

Perhaps late afternoon would be better for photographing that rock, while early morning may be perfect for capturing the strongest shadow of that palm tree.

If you want a panoramic shot of the beach, give it a sense of perspective by framing it with foreground objects, like trees or rocks. Placing a person or an object in the picture will also provide a sense of scale.

Be careful not to underexpose your beach pictures. Often, in extreme lighting situations, your camera exposure meter may not give you a correct reading, so you'll need to compensate by taking a close-up meter reading of your subject. Here's how:

MAKING A CLOSE-UP METER READING

1. Step close to your subject, so that his or her face fills the metering area of your camera or handheld exposure meter completely.
2. Take the meter reading.
3. Move back so that you see more background, and then take a picture at the exposure setting determined by your close-up reading.

Zoo Productions

Andy Caulfield

The photographs above, taken at similar locations, demonstrate how different lighting conditions create different moods. Note how direct sunlight in the photo at the top emphasizes the sunny aspects of the beach, while the afterglow of the sunset captures a romantic mood in the picture below.

PHOTOGRAPHING YOUR VACATION

When you are ready to take a photograph, consider your choice of viewpoints. Taking a picture from high up in your hotel creates an unusual perspective and takes the viewer by surprise.

For a subject in extremely bright light, try increasing your exposure by one stop. If you have an automatic camera that won't allow you to do this, set the film-speed dial at half the speed of the film you're using (for example, set ISO 50 if you're using a 100-speed film).

Don't forget to change the film speed back again when you leave the beach. Change the film-speed setting only to compensate for unusual circumstances, such as extremely bright surroundings. For straightforward shots, stick with the usual setting to avoid overexposure.

TROPICAL ISLANDS

Taking photographs in the tropics can be a real adventure. The flora and fauna are so exotic that you'll want to have lots of film to capture it all.

Colors appear more vibrant in the tropics. Drab scenes are rare; even the houses are painted in bright hues, which makes them fun to photograph.

If you are faced with an extremely contrasty scene—one that includes dark shadows and brilliant sunny areas, for example— study it carefully. Your goal is to get as much detail as possible in the shaded parts without losing the vibrant colors of the sunny areas.

A few simple techniques can help you handle these types of scenes, such as those listed on page 44 under "Forests and Trees." But if all else fails and you just can't get the effect you want, try using the time of day to your advantage. As the sun moves, so do the shadows.

Matthew Loonan

A 50 mm normal lens is all that was needed to capture these beautiful tropical birds in their natural habitat.

PHOTOGRAPHING YOUR VACATION

When you take pictures in the tropics, be aware of vibrant colors, such as this parrot's plumage, that can dominate composition.

Lynn M. Stone

Look for an interplay of colors that will heighten the interest of your pictures, but don't forget about shapes! The angles at which you shoot shapes or forms determine how "three-dimensional" your photographs will look. By studying the colors and shapes of your composition, you'll be able to achieve some outstanding pictures.

Daily rainstorms are typical in the tropics. Although this may cut down on your sun-worshiping hours, why should it stop you from taking pictures? Slip on a slicker and try shooting your environment while it's wet. The rain can give your pictures a lush, exotic flavor. And because fewer people will venture out into the rain, your photos can look as if you had this tropical paradise all to yourself.

Michael O'Connor

In the tropics, even pastel shades take on vibrant hues in direct sunlight.

The sky before and after rainstorms can be very dramatic. Watch for dark, silvery skies before the showers begin and for rainbows and streaks of light filtering through the clouds afterwards.

Always keep your camera as dry as possible when you shoot in the rain, but don't feel you can't use it until the rain has stopped. Keep it shielded in your jacket between shots; then dry it off when you're through. Better still, place your camera in a plastic bag with a hole cut out for the lens—you can keep your camera dry and still manipulate its controls.

The tropics mean heat and humidity. You'll want to be particularly careful about storing your film in a cool, dry place. Avoid using plastic bags for storing film—they can trap moisture. Check your camera supplies regularly to make sure they are not sticky and damp. Packing a few packets of silica gel in your camera bag helps absorb moisture. These packets are sold at most camera stores.

ROCKY SEASHORES

Rocky coastlines in places like the Pacific Northwest (Oregon, Washington, and British Columbia) and Britain tend to have cool weather and many overcast days. They can also be quite windy places with wind-swept terrain.

These coastlines can be breathtakingly beautiful and make great picture subjects. They offer beaches with odd-shaped driftwood and white-capped waves pounding the shores, rocky meadows, craggy cliffs, and the kind of spectacular lighting that a medium-speed film loves. If you take them correctly, your pictures will have strong colors and good detail.

People are also attractive photo subjects in this environment. The bracing weather of the rocky coastline brings out the ruddy-cheeked, fresh-faced look in everyone. Just remember to pose your subjects so that they face into the wind—you'll have a better chance of taking a shot before the wind whips their hair

Hans Wendler

Surf buffeting the coastline provides many dramatic photo opportunities.

David W. Hamilton

Larry Dale Gordon

Not only is the scenic beauty of a rocky coastline an interesting main subject, but it also provides a wonderful backdrop for family portraits.

PHOTOGRAPHING YOUR VACATION

into their faces. If the wind is too strong and is making your subject uncomfortable, have him or her turn away from the wind while you focus or make other adjustments.

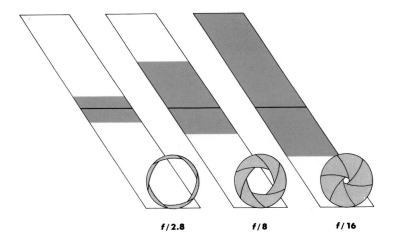

f/2.8   f/8   f/16

This diagram demonstrates how depth of field works. In each example, the camera is focused on the subject. With a wide aperture like f/2.8, the area that will be in focus is shallow. When the lens is stopped down to f/16, a greater area in front of and behind the subject will appear sharp.

If you include scenery in the distance, such as islands or rock formations, you can experiment with just how much you want in focus. This is called controlling *depth of field,* the distance between the nearest and farthest objects that appear in focus. Your depth of field depends on your lens opening (aperture), the focal length of your lens, and the distance from the camera to your subject. For example, if you want the foreground and background to be sharp, you'll have to use a small aperture (*f*/16 or *f*/22, for example). This means, however, that you will probably have to use a slower shutter speed to get the right exposure. If you slow down the shutter speed enough, you may record movement in parts of the scene, such as the ocean.

PEOPLE AND PLACES

DC Productions

SB Productions

These photographs demonstrate how depth of field can affect your photographs. The picture at the top illustrates how great depth of field shows both far and near objects in sharp focus. The picture at left illustrates how shallow depth of field isolates a subject against an out-of-focus background.

Instead of freezing the action, a slow shutter speed will soften the movement, which can make water look silky and smooth.

Be sure to keep an eye out for other moving objects in the frame. Recording the action of the water may be attractive, but a blurred seagull isn't so great.

PHOTOGRAPHING YOUR VACATION

It's not a bad idea to take a tripod—a small, collapsible one—to a windy and wild location, because you could have difficulty holding your camera steady. But if you don't want to bother with a tripod, look for a rock on which to steady your camera.

MOUNTAINS AND VALLEYS

Going high into the mountains and looking down on the valleys below can give you some of the most beautiful vistas in the world. Mountains and valleys provide excellent opportunities to frame distant scenes with objects in the foreground, which gives your pictures a three-dimensional feeling.

You'll find that seasons are quite distinct in the mountains, offering colorful wildflowers in the spring; snow-covered trees in the winter; a carpet of green, rock, and Indian paintbrush in the summer; and a riot of blazing colors in the fall.

Autumn is a favorite season in mountains and valleys, because it brings dramatic color contrasts of changing leaves.

Benn Mitchell

Richard & Mary Magruder

Tall mountains can be snow-capped and chilly even in the summertime. When hiking at high altitudes, carry your camera close to you to keep it warm and operating smoothly.

Burton McNeely

PHOTOGRAPHING YOUR VACATION

When packing for a vacation in the mountains, always include clothes that will be suitable for hiking and photographing in cold as well as warm weather. You may run into weather extremes during whatever season you choose. Even in summer, evenings can get pretty cold, and quite often there's a heavy dew (or even frost) covering the ground in the morning.

Looking down into valleys, you will find lots of trees and possibly foothills. In a scene like this, the sizes of things appear to change, and their colors do as well, as objects fade into the distance. Greens and blues tend to dominate the environment. Try to find other colors to offset these tones, such as a red barn on a hillside. Include wildflowers in bold and beautiful reds, yellows, and oranges.

The colors in some mountain scenes may blend together. Keep your eye out for colors to add contrast and highlight an otherwise monochromatic scene.

Grant Faint

You can reduce haze and reflections from nonmetallic surfaces and enhance color saturation by using a polarizing filter. A polarizer will also darken blue skies photographed at right angles to the sun. However, if you do use a polarizer, you must increase your exposure by 1 1/2 stops. Adjust an automatic camera manually, if possible, because the meter may not give you a correct reading through the filter.

Most polarizing filters consist of an outer ring and an inner ring. To get the effect you want, follow this procedure:

USING A POLARIZING FILTER

1. For maximum darkening of a blue sky, position yourself at a right angle to the sun (one shoulder toward the sun) when the sun is fairly low in the sky.
2. If you have a single-lens-reflex camera, attach the filter to your lens. As you look through the viewfinder, rotate the outer ring until you see the effect you want. With a non-SLR camera, look directly through the filter as you rotate it. When you see the effect you want, keep the filter in the same orientation as you place it over the camera lens.
3. Take the picture!

You can use a skylight filter (No. 1A) with daylight color-slide films to reduce a bluish cast in pictures of scenic views and in photos made on overcast days or in the shade. It requires no increase in exposure.

At higher altitudes, where snow, rocks, and streams prevail, and the dwindling of color creates an overall monochromatic landscape, find the texture of the scene, as well as shadow play. Look for bold shapes and outlines that would make a striking picture.

Lighting and composition can be a challenge. Basic exposure in bright sunlight at altitudes below 2000 feet is the same as for average scenes on the ground. At higher altitudes (2000 to

PHOTOGRAPHING YOUR VACATION

Mountains are dramatic subjects that can challenge your creativity. This photograph transforms a huge three-dimensional mountain into a graphic portrayal of color and form.

Joseph Brignolo

4000 feet), use 1/2 stop less exposure; over 4000 feet, reduce exposure by a full stop.

When photographing your subjects in scenes that include snow, be careful not to get so close in that dirty snow becomes obvious in the picture. Follow the advice on page 65 for proper exposure when snow is everywhere.

As in all locations, experiment with camera angles. The more variety you bring to your pictures, the better.

FORESTS AND TREES

The old adage of not being able to see the forest for the trees applies to photography, too. If the terrain is flat, you may see only large trees in the immediate foreground and miss the greater expanse. And in heavily forested areas, you will have to deal with dark shadows. Although shadows can look dramatic to the eye, capturing them on film so that they reveal all the detail your eye sees is another matter.

Trees can be dramatic subjects in particular types of light—*sidelighting,* for example. When the sun strikes trees from the side, they are infused with light and cast interesting shadows. Backlighting also creates dramatic effects. For successful pictures, however, the sun should be fairly low so that it doesn't completely overpower your subject.

Harold Sund

Sun streaming through trees can heighten the drama of a photograph and relieve the strong vertical lines of the tree trunks.

Always explore the area you plan to photograph, and consider all the different ways of tackling it. Good angles will present themselves if you look hard enough—close-ups, panoramas, the *ant's-eye view* (looking up from very close to the ground), and even aerial shots (if you can get to a higher elevation).

Framing and composition deserve particular attention when you're shooting in the woods. So much of what you'll see is vertical (at first glance, anyway) that it may be difficult to achieve a balanced composition. Take time to examine the entire field of view carefully to find horizontals (the outward thrust of pine boughs) and diagonals (fallen trees) that may not be immediately apparent.

When you are relatively close to your subject, you can brighten dark shadows by using flash or by using a reflector to bounce sunlight into the shadows. This doesn't mean that you have to pack professional gear like silver-lined umbrellas. You

By getting down on the ground and shooting from a low angle, the photographer created a different and interesting viewpoint.

Brett Froomer

Colin Molyneux

All forests don't have to look alike. By shooting from a distance, you can get an overview of the entire forest as in the picture at left; by stepping closer, you can concentrate on the many colors and patterns in a single tree.

Shinzo Maeda

PHOTOGRAPHING YOUR VACATION

can use just about anything with a light surface, such as white paper or a piece of light-colored cloth. Hold the reflector so that the sunlight will strike it and be directed onto your subject. If you're making close-up shots with the sun directly overhead, try placing the reflector on the ground to bounce light up into the shadows.

It's always a good idea to try a number of lighting angles when you're shooting. With improvised techniques like these, you may not get it right in the first shot.

Once you've found a scene that inspires you, size it up carefully. Even though you're out in the woods, you can still run across unattractive clutter like power lines, telephone poles,

The snow-laden leaves in this picture create a bright horizontal contrast to the dark vertical bark of the trees.

Gary Chapman

garbage cans, and signposts. Power lines, in particular, can be a problem. They never look too offensive when you're taking the picture, but later on you'll see awkward horizontal streaks across an otherwise beautiful, natural scene in your prints or slides.

Experiment by bracketing your exposures (taking additional photos with more and less exposure than indicated by your meter reading) if possible. If your meter indicates 1/250 second at f/16, for example, take two other shots—one at 1/125 second and one at 1/500 second. When you get your photos back, choose which exposure you like best.

Also experiment with depth of field. Perhaps a soft, out-of-focus background—such as that produced by using a large aperture like f/2.8—would complement a striking foreground subject.

PARKS AND PRESERVES

Think of a park as a visual puzzle, and ask yourself what the important pieces are. Could it be a famous spot like Old Faithful in Yellowstone? Is the park renowned for its splendid waterfalls or brilliant foliage in the fall?

No matter what park you're photographing, it helps to get there early so that you can take photographs without having to deal with crowds.

It may be difficult to get the angle you want. In some parks and preserves, rangers have fenced off certain areas to protect them or to prevent injury to tourists. If you can't climb just a little bit into the Grand Canyon to get that view you know will be spectacular, you will just have to try a different approach.

Why not experiment with lighting? When you photograph landscapes, look for attractive sources of light. Get there early and leave late to see how the landscape changes dramatically from dawn to dusk.

Take advantage of seasonal changes as well. Winter, for example, gives you weak light (augmented perhaps by the reflective surface of snow); summer light is harsh and strong; and in the

PHOTOGRAPHING YOUR VACATION

Nature in its serenity presents ample and splendid photo opportunities, such as the waterfall at the right and the complex interweaving of the tree limbs below.

Harald Sund

Marvin E. Newman

fall and spring, light tends to be bright and cheery. Keep all these things in mind when you're buying film: you may need to use different films for the different types of light you'll encounter. (See film chart on page 14.)

While parks and preserves offer beautiful and often uninterrupted landscapes, you'll also find large expanses of uninterrupted sky. Although this can give your picture a great deal of scope and the feel of wide-open spaces, you must develop an instinct for "ducking"—aiming your camera a little lower than you would ordinarily. This will prevent your pictures from being full of sky and little else.

Also aim low when the sky is overcast. Try camera angles that exclude most of the sky, unless a dark sky is particularly appealing.

Gabriel / M. Covian

When you compose your photograph, let your subject be the key to its framing. Although trees are not usually seen as horizontal subjects, the sweep of these low branches would have been lost in a vertical shot.

If you shoot nearby subjects with a bright sky as the background, the technique is called *backlighting*. Unless you want the nearby subjects to appear as silhouettes, you'll need to make a close-up exposure reading of your principal subject (as described on page 29)—whether it's a log cabin, an animal, or a wildflower. Sunset or sunrise is the best time to use the backlighting from direct sun, because it's low enough to be partly obscured by the people or objects in your picture.

When the sun strikes your subject from the side, you have sidelighting. This lighting angle works well with landscapes, because it casts dramatic shadows and reveals forms and textures.

Silhouetting a backlighted subject can add drama to your photographs.

Steve Satushek

If you want to photograph a beautiful sunset, you'll be pleased to know that exposure isn't critical. In fact, a number of exposure settings will work, depending on the mood you want to create. To record the sky at the brightness you see, take a meter reading of the sky and clouds—not the sun itself. Less exposure will give you darker, richer, more dramatic effects.

When the sun is partly or wholly obscured—by a cloud, for example—try one or two stops more exposure than for the sunset. When you want to capture the afterglow of a sunset, try two to four stops more exposure than for the sunset.

Rainbows require no special exposure. Just set your exposure as you normally would, unless you include a large expanse of relatively bright sky in the scene. In this case, base your ex-

Gerald Brimacombe

Taking photographs when the sun is low in the sky, as in this sidelit view of Mt. Rushmore, can flush your subject with warm tones and create dramatic shadows.

PHOTOGRAPHING YOUR VACATION

Correct framing can lift your photographs from the ordinary to the spectacular. The immensity of the canyon at the right and the tranquility of the panoramic lake scene below are enhanced by careful framing.

John P. Kelly

William Logan

_____ 53

Janeart Ltd.

When you take pictures in a park or preserve, don't be so awed by nature's beauty that you forget your family! You'll want a record of the time you spent together.

posure on the foreground. Avoid overexposure, which lightens the colors of the rainbow.

Once you have decided what natural wonders to document and feel you have done them justice, branch out and photograph things that will give your pictures a personal touch: a squirrel snacking on your picnic crumbs or a sing-along around a campfire will add humor and warmth to your photo collection.

Do not, however, try to take photos of wild and potentially dangerous animals—such as grizzly bears—up close. Either use a telephoto lens or stay in your car and photograph through the window.

PHOTOGRAPHING YOUR VACATION

CITIES AND SKYLINES

Cities can really excite your creative instincts. So much is happening: bustling crowds, sidewalk merchants, and street performers are vibrant candid subjects.

You can photograph a city in many ways, recording intimate street scenes, aerial views, architectural details, and more.

Start with your arrival. If you are traveling by plane, you can get spectacular shots—particularly when visibility is good—if you have a window seat. Before you start shooting, ask your flight attendant the current altitude and then gauge your camera settings accordingly. Follow the same exposure advice given for mountain scenes on page 42. Because the plane will be vibrating, avoid resting your arms or camera on the seat or window, and use a high shutter speed (1/250 second above 1000 feet; 1/500 second at lower altitudes).

Jake Rajs

Cities are perfect for panoramic shots. This photograph of New York City shows the diversity of a metropolitan skyline.

Whether you are traveling by train, plane, or car, a polarizing filter will help cut down on reflections when you shoot through windows.

Hilly cities, such as San Francisco, make photography easy, because you can shoot down from many vantage points. But New York City, known more for its tall buildings than its natural terrain, also offers terrific views. Many of New York's skyscrapers, such as the Empire State Building and the twin towers of the World Trade Center, have observation decks from which you can capture breathtaking views.

When you shoot from the top of a skyscraper, always check the visibility ahead of time and carefully plan what time of day is best for shooting. Taking pictures in the late afternoon is better than doing so at high noon. The strong midday sun eliminates detail-enhancing shadows and makes cityscapes look flat.

If the weather is bad, you can still get some beautiful shots if you're below the cloud cover. As in the tropics, rain brings life and shine to dull surfaces like roads and roofs.

Erin Hennessey

Part of the charm of old cities is a sense of timelessness. One way to capture the history of a place is to eliminate all modern elements.

Michael Schneps

Juxtaposing the past with the present is always an interesting
theme, as shown in this picture of last century's architecture braced
by contemporary towers.

Michael Quackenbush

David W. Hamilton

Cities mean more than just tall buildings. Photograph green spots, such as the park at the top, as well as interiors, such as this cavernous train station, to get a well-rounded perspective. And remember to include the people!

PHOTOGRAPHING YOUR VACATION

Weinberg/Clark

A city at night is entirely different from a city during the day. This time exposure made at night portrays cars as streaming lights.

Architecture can be particularly eye-catching, but you may have difficulty framing entire buildings in your viewfinder. If you can't get far enough away, try getting down on the ground and shooting up, or use a wide-angle lens. Also explore other angles, such as framing a building through an archway, shooting reflections in puddles or windows, and narrowing in on a small area to represent the whole structure.

If you're shooting architectural detail, you'll want everything in sharp focus, so use a small aperture for good depth of field. If you must use a slow shutter speed, steady your camera with a tripod or brace it on a wall or railing. Sidelighting enhances details, such as a heavily carved cathedral door or a bas-relief. And if you want to give even richer detail to the picture, under-exposing by one stop may help you achieve this.

People give cities flavor and color. You can capture the dynamic feeling of a large city by taking pictures at a busy terminal during rush hour. Why not snap a picture of the tops of people's heads as they hurry to catch their trains? Such a photo can be a real reminder of what it was like to experience big-city life.

Jake Rajs

Special filters, such as the star filter used for taking this photograph, add an artistic touch.

Shooting a city at night—capturing the romance and excitement of the place after sundown—is a real challenge. You'll need a fast film, such as KODACOLOR GOLD 1600 Film, and a little patience. One picture of a night scene isn't enough. Take several shots at different exposure settings to make sure you get an image that captures the look you're after. A star filter will give an added sparkle to city lights.

Photographing the bright lights of the city can also be a challenge. Moving cars, for example, can turn into dramatic streams of light if you use a medium-speed film and shoot with a slow shutter speed such as 1 second at f/16. (You'll need a tripod for this technique.) For stationary lights, like the neon signs in Las Vegas, a very-high-speed film such as KODACOLOR GOLD 1600 Film will let you make hand-held exposures. Try 1/125 second at f/5.6, and bracket your exposures.

If your camera has a built-in flash, using a high-speed film will extend the flash range, so you can take outdoor flash pictures at night. Check your camera manual for flash ranges for films of different speeds, and keep your subject within the correct range.

TOURIST ATTRACTIONS

Visiting tourist attractions and famous sites like Disneyland or our nation's capital gives photographers the chance to take straightforward, picture-postcard shots of well-known places. But just because they're traditional subjects doesn't mean that you can't take creative photos. No matter how conventional the scene is, you can enhance it with good planning, good lighting, and careful framing. The Jefferson Memorial, for example, is a lot more striking when the cherry trees are in bloom. Many monuments look much better at night, when they're dramatically lit by spotlights and few people are in the scene.

Less conventional views—such as a bunch of colorful balloons—are fun. And be sure to photograph your family's enjoy-

Shooting with a wide-angle lens from an unusual viewpoint made this very typical subject look atypical.

Robert Phillips

When you visit an amusement park, look for subjects that emphasize its friendliness, festivity, and energy.

PHOTOGRAPHING YOUR VACATION

Using a large aperture for shallow depth of field lets you isolate your subjects from crowded or cluttered backgrounds.

Jan Somma

ment of the moment with props that identify the location—such as a novelty hat or perhaps a sign on a famous street corner.

Family members personalize any picture. But along with your family, hundreds of other families come to enjoy the sights. As the photographer, you can do two things to help keep them out of your picture, or at least make them less obvious.

One approach is to shoot your subject from a low angle to minimize a problem background. Another is to limit background clutter by choosing a relatively large aperture (and a correspondingly faster shutter speed) to limit depth of field and place greater emphasis on your main subject.

PART THREE

TYPES OF VACATIONS

John P. Kelly

The type of vacation you choose tells as much about you as the photos you take. For example, if you're the kind of person who enjoys lots of activity, you'll want your pictures to record your feats as well as your fun! But if you just like to rent a house and relax, you still want photos that reflect the good times and leisurely pace.

In Part Three, we'll discuss several types of vacations, the kinds of equipment you'll need for typical situations, and tips on how to get the best pictures possible.

SKIING

Skiing is a terrific sport, but it's also hardware-heavy. Ski poles, heavy gloves, cold weather—none of these makes taking pictures easy!

So take a camera that's easy to use in a strong carrying case with a comfortable strap for your neck. You may want to invest in an elastic camera harness that you can strap to your chest, or a photographer's vest, which will help you carry your equipment and film safely and comfortably.

However you decide to carry your camera, keep it and your film close to your body to keep everything warm. That way, the film won't get brittle and break when you advance or rewind it; also, keeping film warm helps prevent static electricity, which can leave marks on film.

You will find the winter sun reflecting off snow and ice everywhere. Your exposure meter may be fooled by bright snow scenes and indicate too little exposure. To be safe, always take at least one shot of the scene at a setting one stop over the meter reading. Also, a polarizing filter can help reduce reflections from airborne moisture to give more saturated colors. Follow the steps for controlling exposure in the mountains, page 42.

Snow itself can be a compelling subject for a photograph. Snow tends to give a soft, blurry appearance to pastel shades, and snowflakes at night are particularly beautiful when you photograph them with flash.

When composing your shot, look for viewpoints that offer contrast, like hard rocks and soft clouds. This will also help give your skiing pictures a sense of place, complementing those pictures that show only white snow.

If you want to take action shots of people skiing, you can pre-focus your camera and set it for a fast-action situation so that you won't miss the shot as the activity gets close. Set the smallest aperture and highest shutter speed that the lighting conditions will allow, and then focus on a spot where most of the action will take place.

Take your pictures from a viewpoint where the subjects are moving toward or away from you. Subjects photographed this way show less motion relative to the camera than subjects going by at a right angle, so you can "stop" the action more easily in your pictures. Also, the farther away the subject is, the easier it is to freeze it. It's difficult to avoid blurred pictures when you photograph very fast action close up.

Another way to shoot fast action is to pan your camera with the subject. To do this, move your camera smoothly to keep

John P. Kelly

Be very careful not to underexpose your photographs when you are surrounded by snow.

PHOTOGRAPHING YOUR VACATION

It's easy to show the excitement of movement either by using a fast shutter speed to freeze the action, as in the photograph at the right, or by panning your camera with the subject, as in the photo below.

David Brownell

Michael Salas

TYPES OF VACATIONS

your subject centered in the viewfinder as you squeeze the shutter release. The subject will be sharp and the background blurred, giving the picture the look of action. Practice this technique until you feel truly comfortable with it.

BOATING AND UNDERWATER SPORTS

Out on the water in a sailboat, a kayak, or a motorboat, you'll find everything from action shots to tranquil scenes.

Brightly painted boats reflected in the water reveal an ever-changing abstract composition. And moving water is always interesting, whether you shoot only the water and reflections, or introduce other subjects. For the clearest reflections, shoot in the early morning or evening, when the sun is low and the water is still.

When you compose your shot, ask yourself whether you want more sky or water in the picture. You can emphasize a great expanse by having more sky, or great depth by putting more water in your picture.

Many of the tips in earlier chapters apply to making photos out on the water. For example, treat water sports like any other fast action; pre-set your camera and wait for the peak of the action.

Dan Esgro

Tom King

Water can look active or passive in a photograph. Capturing objects mirrored in calm water at the water-line is relatively easy. However, water in motion, such as the wake made by the churning motorboat above, or the arc of water made by the water-skier at the right, is harder to predict.

Janeart Ltd.

69

If the opportunity presents itself, try a little underwater photography. The colors of tropical fish and the experience of taking pictures in itself can be an exciting challenge.

Light can be harsh out on the water, so take an extra shot with one stop more exposure in case your camera meter is fooled by the light reflecting off the water.

When you take your camera out on the water, be sure it is in a sturdy case. When you're not taking pictures, keep it in a shady, cool place, along with your extra film.

Guard against humidity and damp by including one or two packets of silica gel in your camera bag to absorb moisture. (Renew or dry out the packets when necessary to prevent them from becoming saturated.) If fungus does appear on your lens, have it stripped down and cleaned by a professional lens repairer.

Next time you're out on the water, why not take a dive with your camera and try some underwater photography?

Today's technology makes it easy with brightly colored 35 mm cameras that are designed to be used underwater. The bright colors, typically yellow, help you locate the camera in case you lose your grip and it begins to float away. You can use most of these cameras at depths to 16 feet. Most have autofocus and built-in flash.

PHOTOGRAPHING YOUR VACATION

Another way to get started shooting underwater is to rent or buy an underwater housing for your present camera. Housings made of metal or plastic let you use just about any 35 mm camera with through-the-lens viewing for underwater photography.

Once you're below the surface, keep your eye on the clarity of the water. Stormy conditions mix sand and silt into the waves and make the water cloudy. If possible, wait until the water is calm before taking pictures.

The level of light decreases the farther down you go, so unless you plan to take pictures just below the surface, use a fast film, such as KODACOLOR GOLD 400 Film. Then increase the normal above-water exposure by 1 1/2 stops just under the surface, by 2 stops at 6 feet, and by 2 1/2 stops at 20 feet.

CLIMBING AND CAMPING

Some of the most intimate and humorous picture opportunities occur on climbing and camping trips. The scenery is spectacular and worth documenting, but don't forget those happy campers working up a sweat or cooking in the great outdoors.

Photographs of camping and hiking scenes often reflect a subject's communion with nature.

Robin Forbes

Janeart Ltd.

Have your camera handy for spontaneous fun, whether it's moments with your family or encounters with the environment.

PHOTOGRAPHING YOUR VACATION

People tend to lose their self-consciousness and let their guard down on this kind of trip, giving you a chance to take satisfying candid portraits.

Travel light and have your camera handy at all times. If you're climbing at high altitudes, follow the advice on page 42 for correct exposure. If you camp deep in the woods, remember to follow the advice on pages 44 through 48.

Everything from wildlife to picnics to "berrying" with your travelling companions will be worth documenting as you march through the woods and up the hills.

TOURING AND SIGHTSEEING

A change of environment stimulates us. It helps us take a fresh look at subjects and situations. You don't to have to go far to get a fresh perspective—it can be as easy as visiting the seashore for a weekend.

Grant Faint

Take pictures of the subjects for which your vacation spot is known. Don't overlook major attractions because you feel they're too obvious.

Faustino

Cliff Feulner

Capture that moment that sums up your vacation in a single picture, whether it's the greeting of a hula dancer or a Viking ship sailing up the Thames.

Photographing the people of a region, particularly if they wear a distinctive style of dress, helps convey the atmosphere of a place. And if you're friendly and "up front" about taking people's portraits, you shouldn't have any problem. Always be sure to ask permission when you photograph individuals.

Look at what's special about the place and what brings you

PHOTOGRAPHING YOUR VACATION

the most enjoyment. Places are photogenic for all kinds of reasons. An outdoor café on the streets of Paris, for example, is a lovely place to sit and snap the world going by; the awesome solitude of the pyramids of Chichén Itzá may inspire you to take outstanding scenes.

You may want to use a telephoto lens to take candid pictures in local settings. Some of the greatest photojournalists in the world, however, have shot great street scenes with a normal lens. To do this, you've got to be in the thick of things, with your camera ready at all times—sometimes it's a matter of being athletic, and sometimes it's being in the right place at the right time.

THE VACATION HOUSE

Whether you're staying in a big old lodge or in a cozy cabin, you'll want to take home a few memories of your vacation house. Interior shots can be tricky, particularly if you must work in low light with reflecting surfaces and furnishings that don't necessarily match.

Interiors may be lighted by natural daylight coming through a window or door, artificial tungsten light (regular household bulbs), fluorescent fixtures, or a combination of sources.

The color quality of tungsten light is different from that of

Ira Block

Photographs of your vacation home should reflect both your fond memories and the flavor of the surroundings you chose.

If you must use flash for proper exposure, try using bounce flash to supplement the existing light while maintaining a natural look. If you can tilt the flash head or separate the unit from the camera, aim it at the ceiling or a nearby light-colored wall.

PHOTOGRAPHING YOUR VACATION

daylight. If you're not supplementing the existing light with flash, it's a good idea to use a tungsten slide film such as KODAK EKTACHROME 160 Film Tungsten or a daylight film with a No. 80A filter to avoid an orange cast. Daylight color print films such as KODACOLOR GOLD 400 and 1600 Films normally give good results under existing tungsten light, because color balance can be adjusted during printing of the negatives.

Pictures taken on either daylight or tungsten films under fluorescent light usually have a green cast unless you use filters.

You may have to use a fairly slow shutter speed and wide aperture for proper exposure in low light (for example, f/2.8 at 1/60 second). At shutter speeds slower than 1/30 second, use a tripod or other camera support.

Using the existing light in the room will give you a more natural look than flash, which may overexpose nearby objects and underexpose the background.

Try not to shoot toward your light source, because objects in the room may appear as silhouettes. Take advantage of natural reflectors outdoors, such as sand or snow, which can bounce light into the room and make dark ceilings and walls more visible.

Avoid including shiny surfaces like mirrors, windows, tiles, or shiny wood in flash pictures. The flash will reflect from these surfaces straight back to the camera lens and produce glare and reflections. To avoid this, shoot at an angle to these surfaces.

Large interiors provide their own set of challenges. If you want the whole room in the picture, you'll probably have to use a wide-angle lens. If you don't have a wide-angle lens, try a different vantage point such as a loft or balcony.

CONCLUSION. If you follow the suggestions in *Photographing Your Vacation,* your camera should soon feel like an old friend.

As you experiment, not all of your pictures will turn out perfectly. But as you progress, you'll soon be making photographs you can be proud of.

GLOSSARY OF TERMS

Angle of view—The extent of the area "seen" by a lens.

Ant's-eye view—The point of view used to photograph an object from a low angle—for example, a tall building from the ground nearby.

Aperture—Lens opening. The opening in a lens system through which light passes. The size is either fixed or adjustable. Lens openings are expressed as *f*-numbers.

Autofocus—Used to describe cameras that focus automatically on the subject when you aim the camera so that the subject is within the autofocus marks or brackets in the viewfinder.

Automatic flash unit—A flash unit with a sensor that measures the light reflected from a scene or the light at the film plane and shuts off when the proper amount of light has been emitted.

Backlighting—Light shining on the subject from the direction opposite the camera.

Bird's-eye view—The point of view used to photograph an object from above—for example, an aerial view of a tall building.

Bounce flash—A technique in which flash is directed at (or "bounced" off) a large reflective surface to provide softer, more diffused illumination.

Bounce lighting—Bouncing light from a flash unit or a photolamp off the ceiling or wall to produce a more even, natural effect.

Bracketing—Making extra photographs at exposure settings to provide more and less exposure than the calculated or recommended setting—for example, at +1, +2, –1, and –2 stops from the calculated setting.

Built-in flash unit—A non-detachable unit that is a part of some camera models. It is usually turned on by a button, but some units will automatically activate when the meter determines that the scene is too dark for proper exposure without flash.

Candid pictures—Unposed pictures of people, often taken without the subject's knowledge.

Color balance—The ability of a film to reproduce the colors of a scene accurately. Color films are balanced during manufacture for exposure to light of a certain color quality: daylight, tungsten, etc.

Color temperature—A measurement of the color quality of light sources; expressed in degrees Kelvin (K).

Composition—The arrangement of all elements in a picture: main subject, foreground, background, and supporting subjects.

Contrast—The range of densities in a photograph; the brightness range of a subject or the lighting in a scene.

Conversion filters—Filters used to balance film to a light source different from the source for which it is designed.

Daylight-balanced film—Film that has been balanced to produce accurate color rendition in daylight or with electronic flash.

Depth of field—The distance between the nearest and farthest object in a scene that appear in acceptable focus in a photograph.

Diffusion—Softening of detail in a photograph by using a diffusion filter or other material that scatters light.

Diffusion filter—A type of filter that diffuses light. Diffusion filters come in varying strengths.

Direct flash—Flash that strikes the subject directly.

Electronic flash—A brief but intense burst of light from the flashtube of a built-in or detachable flash unit; used to supplement existing light or provide the main light on the subject.

Existing light—In photography, existing light is the light that is already on the scene, and includes light from room lamps, fluorescent lamps, spotlights, neon signs, candles, daylight coming through windows, twilight, and moonlight.

Exposure—The amount of light that acts on a photographic material; a product of the intensity (controlled by the lens opening) and the duration (controlled by the shutter speed) of light striking the film or paper.

Exposure meter—An instrument—either built into a camera or a separate, hand-held unit—that measures the intensity of light; used to determine the aperture and shutter speed for proper exposure.

Fill-in flash—Light from a flash unit that is used to brighten shadows created by the primary light source.

Film speed—The sensitivity of a film to light, indicated by a number, such as ISO 200; the higher the number, the more sensitive, or faster, the film.

Film-speed setting—A camera setting—either manual or automatic—that tells the camera the speed of the film.

Filter—A piece of colored glass or other transparent material used over the lens to emphasize, eliminate, or change the color or density of the entire scene or certain elements in the scene.

Flash calculator dial—A control on a flash unit that tells the correct aperture for the camera-to-subject distance, or the correct distance range for a particular aperture.

Flash-synchronization (sync) shutter speed—The speed at which the camera shutter is synchronized with the firing of the flash.

Flashtube—The gas-filled tube that emits a short, intense burst of artificial light.

f-number or f-stop—A number used to indicate the size of the opening on most camera lenses. Common f-numbers are f/2, f/2.8, f/4, f/5.6, f/8, f/11, f/16, and f/22. The higher the f-number, the smaller the lens opening.

Focal length—The distance from the optical center of a lens to the film plane when the lens is focused at infinity.

Freezing action—A technique that makes an object in motion appear "stopped"; can be accomplished by using a high shutter speed or electronic flash.

Frontlighting—Light that strikes the subject from the front.

Hot shoe—The fitting on the camera that holds a portable flash unit. It provides electrical contact with the base of the flash unit so that the flash fires when you press the shutter release.

ISO speed—A system of the International Organization for Standardization for measuring film speed.

Lens—One or more pieces of optical glass or similar material designed to collect and focus rays of light to form a sharp image on the film or paper.

Lens aperture—see "Aperture."

Manual exposure control—A camera exposure system that allows the photographer to adjust aperture and shutter speed manually.

Manual flash—A flash unit that emits the same amount of light each time it fires. It has no sensor to measure and adjust the amount of light.

Normal lens—A lens that produces an image with perspective similar to that of the original scene. A normal lens has a longer focal length and narrower field of view than a wide-angle lens, and a shorter focal length and wide angle of view than a telephoto lens.

Off-camera flash—Using a flash unit off the camera to provide sidelighting, bounce lighting, or other indirect illumination.

Overexposure—A situation in which too much light reaches the film, producing a dense negative or a light slide.

Panning—Moving the camera during exposure to follow a moving subject.

Point-and-shoot camera—An automatic non-SLR camera, usually with built-in flash.

Polarizing filter—A filter that blocks polarized light; can be used to darken a sky or eliminate reflections from nonmetallic surfaces.

Rangefinder—A focusing device on non-SLR cameras. It shows the photographer two images of the subject that must be aligned for proper focus.

Red-eye—A phenomenon caused by reflection of the flash by blood vessels in the back of the eye.

Reflector—Any device used to reflect light onto a subject.

Reflected-light meter—An exposure meter used to measure the amount of light reflecting from a subject.

Sidelighting—Light striking the subject from the side relative to the position of the camera.

Silica gel—A highly absorbent material used as a drying agent.

Skylight (UV) filter—Used to cut through haze and eliminate the blue cast often seen in scenics or photographs made in open shade.

Single-lens-reflex (SLR) camera—A camera that uses a prism and mirror to provide viewing through the picture-taking lens.

Soft focus—Produced by use of a special filter to soften an image.

Star filter—A filter with crossed horizontal and vertical lines etched into its surface that makes specular light sources look like stars.

Stop(s)—Exposure settings are measured in stops. Each single-increment change in shutter speed or aperture represents one stop, and halves or doubles the amount of light striking the film. (Also see "f-stop.")

Sync (synchronization) cord—An extension cord that connects the camera to a flash unit to provide electrical contact and synchronization with the shutter.

Telephoto lens—A lens that creates a larger image of the subject than a normal lens at the same camera-to-subject distance.

Three-quarters lighting—Light striking the subject at a 45-degree angle from the line between the subject and the camera.

Through-the-lens meter (TTL)—A built-in camera meter that determines exposure for the scene by reading the light that passes through the lens.

Tungsten-balanced film—Film that has been balanced to produce accurate color rendition under tungsten light.

Tungsten light—Light from normal household lamps and ceiling fixtures (not fluorescent).

Underexposure—A condition in which too little light reaches the film, producing a thin negative or a dark slide.

Viewfinder—A camera viewing device that shows the subject area that will be recorded on the film.

Wide-angle lens—A lens that covers a wider field of view than a normal lens at the same subject distance.

Zoom lens—A variable-focal-length lens that can be used in place of a number of individual fixed-focal-length lenses.

GLOSSARY

INDEX

Aerial photography, 11, 45, 55, **55**, 56
Aperture: for beach photographs, **28**; for bounce-flash, 26; definition, 21; depth of field and, 37, 59, 63, **63**; exposure control and, 21, 23–24; *f*-numbers, 23; for movement photographs, 66

Beaches, photographing of, 27–31, **27**, **30**
Boating vacations, photographing of, 68–71, **68, 69**

Camera: care of, 27, 34, **40**, 65, 70; control adjustments, **12**; manual for, 11; self-timer, **22**; for underwater photography, 70–71
Camping vacations, photographing of, 71–73, **71, 72**
Candid photographs, 21, 75
Cities, photographing of, 55–60, **55, 56, 57, 58, 59, 60, 61**, 75
Climbing vacations, photographing of, 71–73
Color: composition and, 32–34, **33, 34**; in mountains, 39, **39**, 41, **41**, 42
Composition: of beach photographs, 28, 29, **29, 31**; color and, 32–34, **33, 34**; of forest photographs, 45; of mountain/valley photographs, 43; of snow photographs, 66; of water photographs, 68

Depth of field, 14, 37, 48, 59, 63, **63**

Equipment, insurance for, 10; packing of, 11
Exposure: for aerial photographs, 55; for beach photographs, 28, 29, 31; bracketing of, 48; control of, 21, 23–24; in mountains, 42, 43; for night photography, **59**, 60, **60**, 61; for rainbows, 52, 54; in snow, 43, 65; for sunsets, 52; for underwater photography, 71
Expressions, of family members, 21
Eyes, reflections from, 25–26

Film: airport X-ray inspection of, 16, 19; care of, 34, 65; choice of, 9; for different light conditions, 13–15, **13, 14, 15, 16**, 50; mailing of, 19; for night photography, 60; "process before" date, 16; processing of, 19; purchase of, 13–16; speed dial setting, 31; tungsten slide, 77; for underwater photography, 71
Filter: to prevent green cast, 77; polarizing, 9, 42, 56, 65; skylight, 42; star, 60, **60**
Forests, photographing of, 44–48, **44, 45, 46, 47**
Framing, 45, **53**

Groups, photographing of, 24–25, **25**

Kodak Information Center, 19

Lens: care of, 27, 70; telephoto, 14, 54, 75; wide-angle, 24–25, **25**; for wildlife photography, **32**; zoom, 14, **25**
Lighting: backlighting, 44, 51, 51; for

beach photographs, 27, 28–31, **30**; exposure control, 21, 23–24; film types and, 13–15, **13, 14, 15, 16**, 50; flash (bounce-flash, 26, **76**; range, 25; in forest scenes, 45; outdoors at night, 60); for forest photographs, 45, 47; indoors, 75–77, **76**; for mood, **30**; for mountain photographs, 43; seasonal variations in, 48, 50; sidelighting, 44, 51, 59; tungsten lights, 75, 77
Lights, photographing of 60, **60**
Mountains, photographing of, 39–43, **39, 40, 41, 43, 52**
Movement, photographing of, **69**

Night photography, **59**, 60, **60**, 61

Parks and preserves, photographing of, 48–54, **49**
People, photographing of, 20–26, **20**; on camping trips, **71**, 73; in cities, 59; in parks and preserves, **54**; permission for, 74; of photographer, 21, **22**; on seashores, 35, **36**, 37, **38**; while sightseeing, 74; of skiers, 66, **66, 67**, 68; at tourist attractions, 63

Rain, photographing in, 33–34, 56
Rainbow, photographing of, 52, 54
Reflections: from eyes, 25–26; from shiny surfaces, 42, 77; from snow, 65; through windows, 56
Reflector, 45, 47, 77

Seashores, photographing of, 35, 39, **35, 36, 37, 38**
Shadows, 44, 45
Shutter speed, 21, 23; for aerial photography, 55; for city photography, 59; for movement photography, 66, **67**; for seashore photography, 37–38
Silhouette effect, **17**, 51, **51**, 77
Skiing vacations, photographing of, 65–68, **64, 66, 67**
Snow, photography of/in, 65–66, **66**
Sunsets, photographing of, 52, **52**

Touring and sightseeing, photography while, 73–75, **73, 74, 75**
Tourist attractions, photographing of, 61–63, **61, 62, 63**
Trees, photographing of, 44–48, **44, 45, 46, 47, 49, 50**
Tripod, 39
Tropical islands, photographing of 32–34, **32, 33, 34**

Underwater sports, photographing of, 68–71, **70**

Vacation house, photographing of 75–77, **75, 76**
Valleys, photographing of, 39–43, **39, 40, 53**

Wildlife photography, **32, 33**, 54, **70, 72, 73**

Please note: Entries which appear in bold refer to captions.

PHOTOGRAPHING YOUR VACATION